HAWAII'S SPAM® COOKBOOK

HAWAII'S SPAM® COOKBOOK

including recipes for

- sardines
- corned beef &
- vienna sausage

Ann Kondo Corum

BESS PRESS, INC.
HONOLULU, HAWAII

Library of Congress Catalog Card Number: 87-70924
Corum, Ann Kondo
Hawaii's SPAM® Cookbook
Honolulu, Hawaii: Bess Press, Inc.

Published by:
Bess Press, Inc.
Box 22388
Honolulu, Hawaii 96823

Cover: Ann Kondo Corum
Design: Ann Kondo Corum and Steve Shiraki
Typesetting: Pro Print
Cover Photo: Karen Hamada

ISBN: 0-935848-49-5

Dedication

This book is dedicated to all who hold a special place in their hearts (and bellies) for SPAM®.

SPAM® luncheon meat is a registered trademark for a pork product packed only by Geo. A. Hormel & Co., Austin, MN. 55912.

Unless stated otherwise in the recipes, a can of **SPAM®** refers to a 12 oz. can, a can of corned beef refers to a 12 oz. can, and a can of sardines refers to a 3¾ oz. can.

ACKNOWLEDGEMENTS

I would like to thank those who gave me their recipes and their names for use in this book, especially Diane Ueki, who faithfully called in recipes which she got wherever she could. Also, thanks go out to Van E., Sandy, Steve, Brenda, Karen, Randy, Lolly, Lita, Jan, Charlene, and Mrs. Lorraine for cooking and eating many canned delights. And a very special thank you to Hoagy Gamble of L.H. Gamble Company, Hormel's Hawaii food broker, and to Rich Crane, product manager for SPAM® luncheon meat, George A. Hormel Company, Austin, Minnesota.

A.K.C.

TABLE OF CONTENTS

PREFACE xv

SPAM®

Fried **SPAM**® 2

Kalua **SPAM**® 4

SPAM® Sandwiches 6

SPAM® wich 8

SPAM® Musubi 9

SPAM® Musubi Variations 11

SPAM® and Mushroom Rolls 12

Stuffed Celery 13

Sato-Shoyu **SPAM**® 14

SPAM® Balls 16

SPAM® Toast 17

SPAM® Won Ton 18

Basic **SPAM**®-Fishcake Pupu Mix 19-20

SPAM® Lumpia 22

SPAM® Chowder 24

SPAM® Soup 25

SPAM® Slaw 26

Long Rice/Wakame Salad 28

Somen Salad. 29
SPAM® Pasta Salad 30
SPAM® Fu Young. 32
SPAM® Omelet. 34
SPAM® and Zucchini Omelet 35
SPAM® McLolly 37
SPAM® Quiche. 38
Fried Saimin 40
Gon Lo Mein With SPAM® 41
SPAM® Fried Rice. 43
Chow Fun. 44
Udon Chow 45
SPAM® Sushi 46
Super Macaroni and Cheese. 48
SPAM® and Cauliflower Casserole 50
SPAM® and Beans. 51
Depression Dinner Party Dish 52
SPAM® Noodles. 53
SPAM® and Vegetable Medley. 54
Quick SPAM® Stir Fry 55
SPAM® with Veggies. 56
Tofu Patties 58
Sweet-Sour Tofu and SPAM® 60
Sweet-Sour SPAM®. 61

SPAM® and Eggplant 62
SPAM®, String Beans, and Eggs 64
SPAM® and Popping Peas 65
SPAM® and Peas 66
SPAM® Stuffed Hasu 68
Miso SPAM® With Vegetables 69
SPAM® and Daikon 71
Eggplant (or Zucchini) and SPAM® Tempura 72
Veggie and SPAM® Tempura 74
SPAM® and Kim Chee Chun 75
Korean Style SPAM® 76

CORNED BEEF, SARDINES, AND VIENNA SAUSAGE

Corned Beef and Onions 80
Corned Beef and Onions, Sato-Shoyu 80
Corned Beef, Onions, and Potatoes 81
Quick Corned Beef and Cabbage 83
Fried Corned Beef and Cabbage 84
Corned Beef and Cabbage Salad 85
Corned Beef Spread 86
Corned Beef Sandwich Filling 87
Ice Chest Corned Beef Spread 88
Reuben Sandwich 90

Corned Beef Omelet 91
Corned Beef Hash 92
Mrs. Higuchi's Corned Beef Patties 94
Corned Beef and Vegetable Patties. 94
Papakolea Hawaiian Goulash. 95
Corned Beef Crescents 96
Confetti Corned Beef. 97
Haole Manapua 99
Corned Beef Manapua 100
Creamed Corned Beef 101
Portuguese Tacos. 103
Corned Beef Enchiladas. 104
Corned Beef Noodle Casserole 105
Sardines and Eggs. 107
Lomi Sardine. 108
Sardine Buns. 110
Sardine Spread. 111
Sardines and Onions. 112
Sardines With Somen. 113
Filipino Style Sardines and Long Rice. 114
Tomato Sardine Salad. 114
Sardine Salad. 117
Sardine-Okara Patties 118
Sardine and Tofu. 119

Sardine and Tofu Souffle...120
Mabel's Kim Chee Sardines...121
Sardine and Warabi (Fern Shoots)...................................122
Sardines and Eggplant...123
Sardine-Miso Udon...124
Sardine Ozoni...126
Vienna Sausage Pupus..129
Polka-Dot Pancakes..130
Pokey-Pokey...131
Puukolii Pork 'N' Beans...133

PREFACE

Mention SPAM® in Hawaii and you are bound to get a reaction, usually favorable, for SPAM® is very much a part of Hawaii's food legacy. Hawaii holds the honor of being the SPAM® "capital" of the United States. Local residents consume 4 million cans every year. That comes out to 10,958 cans per day. On a per capita basis, that means we consume approximately 3½ times more SPAM® than any other state. SPAM® is real "local food" . . . it is Hawaii's soul food.

SPAM® is a luncheon meat made by George A. Hormel & Company in Austin, Minnesota. To local residents, SPAM® is SPAM®, and no other luncheon meat can ever be passed off as SPAM®. Developed in 1937, the spiced meat product lacked a catchy name, so the Hormel Company sponsored a contest to name the new luncheon meat. The winning entry, SPAM® (for spiced ham), was submitted by Kenneth Daugneau. He won a prize of $100.00.

Following its birth in the late 1930's, SPAM® gained popularity quickly because of World War II. It became a staple in the diets of troops overseas and people in war torn countries such as England and islands such as Hawaii, which had trouble getting fresh meat. Following the war, G.I.'s returning home tried to forget SPAM®, and it became the brunt of derogatory SPAM® jokes. However, Hawaii continued to consume

SPAM®. Why do we love SPAM®? It could be because it goes so well with rice, our staple starch. Or, it could be because its flavor blends so well with vegetables and noodles. It could also be because it was part of plantation cookery and a regular item in the diets of our parents and grandparents.

Whatever the reason for Hawaii's love affair with SPAM®, there are certain down-home ways of eating SPAM®, like SPAM® 'n' eggs 'n' rice. Or SPAM® musubi, or SPAM® saimin, or SPAM® sandwiches made with white bread. SPAM® even appears on the menus of several local restaurants.

While SPAM® is king of the canned meats in Hawaii, it is followed in popularity by corned beef, Vienna sausages, and sardines. These three items were also a part of plantation cookery, and like SPAM®, they are a continuing part of local food culture. These canned goods are all pre-cooked, keep well on the shelf, taste good with rice, and can be stretched by adding vegetables. And because they are pre-cooked, they are quick and easy to prepare.

When I first got the idea of a SPAM® and other canned meats cookbook, I didn't know if I could even come up with enough recipes to fill an entire book. But, as I talked to people, I realized that there are countless SPAM® and other canned meat recipes because these items are very much a part of local residents' lives. People got really excited, telling me about their recipes, or a friend's mother's sister's recipe! A common feature that stands out in my mind about these recipes is that many are variations of another. Numerous times, specific ingredients were given to me, but no amounts. So I spent many hours measuring and testing the recipes on my "guinea pig" friends and family.

I am sure that I have not included many recipes which abound in this state. There are a few "Haole-type" recipes included, but the majority of the recipes are local style. I know you will love Lloyd Pak's Korean-Style SPAM®. And local folks on the mainland will be delighted with the recipes for Lomi Sardines and Corned Beef Manapua. Ingredients for most of these recipes can be found even in Bismarck, North Dakota. And who knows, maybe some mainland folk (not transplanted locals) will discover this book and realize that there is more to SPAM® than baked SPAM® with brown sugar and more to corned beef than corned beef hash. A glossary of ingredients and local terms used in the book is appended.

There are no complicated recipes in this book. And, while ingredients are listed, there are no hard, fast rules. Pass around these recipes, add new ingredients, substitute your new ideas. Cooking is fun, and hopefully, this cookbook will not only be fun, but it will preserve some of our down-home flavors for future generations. I hope this book makes you smile!

Ann Kondo Corum

Fried SPAM®

The best way to fry **SPAM®** is to fry it in a black cast iron skillet. Fry it until it is almost, but not quite crisp. Some people slice it thick, and others cut it into "logs," but most prefer it sliced about ¼ inch thick.

Fried SPAM® doesn't need any sauce or seasoning, but many SPAM® lovers eat it with a bit of shoyu. Try fried SPAM® on a bed of finely shredded lettuce or cabbage and topped a sauce of mayonnaise and shoyu (Japanese salad dressing) . . . delicious!

Kalua SPAM®

1 can SPAM®
ti leaves

foil
charcoal

Build a charcoal fire in the sand. Wrap SPAM® in ti leaves and then in foil. Place in glowing coals.

This method of cooking SPAM® comes from Carl Higuchi who says this is how he cooks SPAM® at the beach. When you come back from diving, fishing, or surfing, your SPAM® will be hot and ready to eat with musubi! If you have any leftover, use it for bait.

"SPAM® makes good bait."

SPAM® Sandwiches

SPAM®, sliced

mayonnaise
bread, fluffy white kind

Spread slices of bread liberally with mayonnaise; put SPAM® between slices of bread.

True SPAM® afficionados use only WHITE BREAD, but you may use other kind of bread. Add Manoa lettuce if you like. Fried SPAM® (and egg) sandwiches are good too. You can eat SPAM® sandwiches for breakfast, lunch, or dinner. Goes equally well with milk, Coke, or beer!

Man cannot live by bread alone.

7

SPAM® wich

1 can **SPAM®**, cut in thin strips
¼ c. diced green pepper
2 Tbsp. minced onion

1 Tbsp. horseradish
3 Tbsp. mayonnaise
dash of pepper

Combine all ingredients and serve in onion rolls with lettuce, tomatoes, and cheese.

This is a fancy SPAM® sandwich which will impress your friends!

SPAM® Musubi

Cooked rice
ume
SPAM®
nori

Note: Haoles, you must use Calrose rice, not minute rice

Make musubi as usual, except make them oblong (SPAM® shape). Slice SPAM® and fry until brown. Cut nori into strips 2-3 inches wide and long enough to go around the musubi. Place a piece of SPAM® on top and wrap nori around it.

Helpful hint for making SPAM® shaped musubi from the wisdom of Billy Apele: Save your SPAM® can, pat the rice in the can (be careful ... edges of the can are sharp!), and dump it out.

9

"I'll trade you a chicken sandwich and a deluxe super bacon burger for your SPAM® musubi."

10

SPAM® Musubi Variations

SPAM® Musubi Deluxe: Make omelet, Japanese style, place on top of rice, put **SPAM®** on top, and wrap nori around.

Japanese Omelet:

3 eggs
½ tsp. sugar

1 tsp. shoyu
pinch of salt
1 tsp. water

Mix ingredients together with a fork. Put a little oil in a small frying pan. When oil is hot, pour in eggs and cook until set on low heat. Flip eggs out of the pan and cut into rectangles (**SPAM®** shaped).

SPAM® Musubi Supreme: Sprinkle furi-kake nori (seasoned, flaked seaweed) on top of musubi before putting egg and **SPAM®** on it. Use a FULL sheet of nori to wrap the musubi.

Korean Musubi: Season rice with some sesame oil (not too much) and sesame seeds before making musubi.

SPAM® and Mushroom Rolls

¼ c. butter
1 lb. fresh mushrooms, finely chopped
1 c. SPAM®, finely chopped
1 Tbsp. parsley, minced

8 oz. cream cheese, softened
1 loaf sandwich bread, crusts removed
1 cube butter, melted (for brushing on rolls)

Saute mushrooms in butter. Remove from heat and combine with SPAM®, parsley, and cream cheese.
Roll bread slices with a rolling pin, or flatten slices with your hands. Spread bread with cream cheese mixture. Roll like a jelly roll. Cut each roll into 3 pieces and fasten with a toothpick. Brush each roll with the melted butter and place under broiler until brown.

Stuffed Celery

1 can SPAM®, grated
¼ c. onion, minced

3-4 Tbsp. mayonnaise
dash of pepper
celery stalks

Mix grated SPAM®, onion, mayonnaise, and pepper. Cut celery stalks into 2-3 inch lengths and stuff with SPAM®.

Sato-Shoyu SPAM®
(Sugar-Shoyu SPAM®)

SPAM®, sliced or cubed

Sauce:

¼ c. shoyu

¼ c. sugar

¼ c. mirin (Japanese sweet rice wine)

1 tsp. grated ginger

Bring sauce to a boil in a small pan. Add **SPAM®**, lower heat, and cook 2-3 minutes.

Cubed SPAM® cooked this way makes good pupus. Insert toothpicks in the cubes before serving.

"Don't knock it until you've tried it, Honey!"

15

SPAM® Balls

3 c. water
¼ c. milk
½ block margarine
1 tsp. salt
3 c. potato buds

1 can **SPAM®**, grated or minced
3 Tbsp. onion, minced
1 Tbsp. parsley, minced
oil for frying
Panko (Japanese bread crumbs) or
    cornflake crumbs

Heat water, milk, margarine, and salt until bubbly. Remove from heat and add potato buds. Add **SPAM®**, onion, and parsley; mix well. Form small balls and chill until firm. Roll in Panko or cornflake crumbs. Deep fry in oil heated to 350 degrees until golden brown.

Dipping Sauce:

½ c. mirin (Japanese sweet rice wine)

¼ c. shoyu
2 Tbsp. sugar

Combine in a saucepan, bring to a boil, and cool.

SPAM® Toast

1 can **SPAM®**, grated or finely minced
¼ c. onion, minced
½ c. water chestnuts, chopped
2 stalks green onion, sliced
1 egg

½ tsp. pepper
2 tsp. sherry
12 slices sandwich bread, crusts
  removed
oil for frying

Combine all ingredients except bread and oil. Mix well and spread mixture on bread. Cut each slice into 4 pieces. Fry in oil heated to 350 degrees, **SPAM®** side down, until edges begin to brown. Turn and fry until golden. Drain on paper towels.

SPAM® Won Ton

1 can SPAM®, grated or finely minced
½ c. water chestnuts, chopped
2 stalks green onion, sliced
½ tsp. pepper
1 Tbsp. oyster sauce

1 egg
1 Tbsp. cornstarch
1 tsp. sugar
1 pkg. won ton wrappers
oil for frying

Mix all ingredients together (except wrappers and oil). Place a generous teaspoon of the mixture on wrapper and seal edges. Deep fry in oil heated to 350 degrees until won ton is golden brown. Drain on paper towels. Serve with mustard-shoyu.

Mustard-shoyu:
1 Tbsp. dry mustard
1 Tbsp. cold water
2-3 Tbsp. shoyu
Mix all ingredients together until smooth.

How to wrap won ton.

19

Basic SPAM®-Fishcake Pupu Mix

This basic mixture, developed by Mrs. Yee and her daughter, Mrs. Low (two local foodies), may be used in a number of ways. Use your imagination. It makes a lot, so you can serve a big crowd!

1 can **SPAM®**, finely chopped or
  coarsely ground
1 lb. Chinese fishcake
1 Tbsp. oyster sauce

1 Tbsp. sesame oil
1 Tbsp. cornstarch
1 tsp. shoyu
½ tsp. sugar
minced green onion (optional)

Mix all ingredients together and use in one of the following ways, or develop your own ideas.

Mushroom Pupu

Parboil shiitake mushrooms and squeeze them (or use large, fresh mushrooms). Fill with **SPAM®** fishcake mixture and fry in a little oil, **SPAM®** side down. Flip over when lightly browned and cook a few minutes on other side.

Basic SPAM®-Fishcake Pupu Mix (cont.)

Stuffed Aburage

Buy small aburage and cut them in half. Fill with **SPAM®**-fishcake mixture and steam or braise in some chicken broth (canned) for about 20 minutes. Thicken broth with a little cornstarch and water if you want a gravy.

Maki-Nori Pupu

Need: 12-15 sheets sushi nori
Put some pupu mix onto nori sheets and roll into a sushi-like (or jelly roll) roll. Wrap rolls in waxed paper; freeze until solid. Slice into desired thickness and deep fry in oil until brown.

Easy Pupu

Drop pupu mix from a teaspoon into hot oil and fry until brown. Insert toothpicks and serve with mustard-shoyu sauce.

SPAM® Lumpia

1 can SPAM®
1 kamaboko
¼ c. chopped green onion
garlic salt to taste

2 eggs, beaten
1 pkg. chop suey mix, parboiled
1 pkg. lumpia wrappers
oil for frying

Grate or grind **SPAM®** and kamaboko. Mix together with rest of ingredients (except for wrappers and oil). Cool filling. Put 1-2 Tbsp. of filling in center of each wrapper. Fold edge closest to you over filling. Tuck in the two ends. Fold like an envelope. Moisten edges to seal. Heat some oil in a pan and fry lumpia until golden brown. Drain on paper towels.

Sauce:

½ c. catsup
½ c. vinegar
½ c. sugar

1 c. water
1 Tbsp. cornstarch
2 Tbsp. water

Boil catsup, vinegar, sugar, and water together. Mix cornstarch with water and add to the sauce to thicken.

This prize winning recipe was contributed by Vicky Perry, a fabulous cook.

23

SPAM® Chowder

1 medium potato, cubed
1½ c. water
1 c. light cream or evaporated milk
1 can condensed cream of potato soup
¼ c. water

2 Tbsp. cornstarch
dash of pepper
1 can SPAM®, diced
Chopped parsley or green onions for garnish

In a deep saucepan, cook cubed potatoes in 1½ c. water. Do not drain. Combine cream and potato soup in a bowl. Combine water, cornstarch, and pepper in a small dish and stir into the soup mixture. Pour over potatoes and water. Cook, stirring occasionally until thickened and bubbly. Add diced SPAM®. Garnish with parsley or green onions.

SPAM® Soup

1 can SPAM®, cubed
1 (14½ oz.) can of chicken broth
1 can of water
1 onion, cubed

2 stalks celery, sliced
2-3 carrots, sliced
1 potato, cubed
1 box frozen green beans

Place all ingredients, except potatoes and green beans in a pot. Bring to a boil and simmer until carrots are almost done. Add potatoes and cook until they are done. Add green beans last and cook a few minutes. Sprinkle with black pepper and serve.

This recipe comes from Karen Hamada, who reports it is a hot item for tailgate party.

SPAM® Slaw

1 qt. finely shredded cabbage or iceberg lettuce (or a combination of the two)

2 stalks celery, thinly sliced

2 Tbsp. green onion, minced

1 c. SPAM®, sliced into matchstick slivers

¼ tsp. pepper

3-4 Tbsp. mayonnaise

Toss all ingredients together. Serve immediately. Other veggies such as thinly sliced cucumber or coarsely grated carrots may be added.

"And do you, Malia, take this man, Mel, to have and to hold, to love and to cherish, until he refuses to eat SPAM®?"

27

Long Rice/Wakame Salad

1 bundle long rice
1 c. soaked wakame (seaweed), cut in 2
   inch lengths

1 c. finely shredded cabbage
1 carrot, shredded
1 c. **SPAM®**, cut into thin strips
sesame seeds for garnish

Dressing:
5 Tbsp. shoyu
3 Tbsp. Japanese vinegar

2 tsp. sugar
2 tsp. sesame oil

Boil long rice in water for 15 minutes. Drain. Cut into 3 inch lengths. Place in a serving dish and pile the rest of the ingredients on top. Garnish with sesame seeds. Pour dressing on top just before serving.

Somen Salad

1 pkg. somen, cooked as directed on package

head lettuce, shredded

1 kamaboko (fishcake), cut in slivers

1 cucumber, halved and thinly sliced

2 eggs, made into thin omelets, then chopped

1 can **SPAM®**, cut in matchstick slivers

3 stalks green onion, thinly sliced

Lay somen in a large platter or a 9 x 13 inch pan and garnish with other ingredients.

Sauce:

2 Tbsp. sesame seed

2 Tbsp. sugar

¼ c. vegetable oil

1 Tbsp. sesame oil

3 Tbsp. vinegar

2 Tbsp. shoyu

1 Tbsp. sugar

Shake all ingredients together in a jar and pour over salad.

SPAM® Pasta Salad

1 12 oz. bag of pasta (veggie spirals are nice)
¼ medium onion, minced
1 jar (6 oz.) artichoke hearts, including the juice
1 c. chopped cucumber or zucchini

⅓ c. Italian dressing, such as Zesty Italian
½ tsp. salt
¼ tsp. pepper
¼ tsp. oregano
1 c. diced SPAM®

Cook pasta according to package directions. Do not overcook. Rinse with cold water and drain well.

Place all other ingredients in a bowl and mix together. Add drained pasta and toss together. Chill. Decorate top with sliced tomatoes, sliced hard boiled eggs, olives, etc.

Upscale couple stocking up on a staple.

SPAM® Fu Young

½ c. **SPAM®**, slivered
½ c. water chestnuts, slivered
1 small carrot, slivered
1 c. bean sprouts
1 stalk celery, thinly sliced

2 stalks green onions, cut in ½ inch pieces
4 eggs, slightly beaten
½ tsp. shoyu
½ tsp. sugar

Fry **SPAM®** and vegetables in a small amount of hot oil until vegetables are tender, but still crisp. Remove from heat; cool. Season eggs with shoyu and sugar and mix in vegetables and **SPAM®**. Heat a little oil in a pan. Drop 3 Tbsp. of the egg mixture in the pan to make small patties. Fry until brown on both sides over low heat.

SPAM® *a la icebox, a midnight delight.*

SPAM® Omelet

For each omelet:
1 Tbsp. butter
¼ c. diced **SPAM**®

2-3 eggs
1 Tbsp. milk
salt and pepper

Beat eggs, milk, salt and pepper with a fork. Melt butter in a small skillet or omelet pan. When it is sizzling, add **SPAM**® and beaten eggs. Lower heat and cook until almost set. Then lift up one edge of omelet and fold it over.

You can add other ingredients to this basic recipe. Chopped onions, diced green peppers, zucchini, and tomatoes are some possibilities.

SPAM® and Zucchini Omelet

5 Tbsp. butter
⅓ c. sliced mushrooms
1 small zucchini, thinly sliced
1 Tbsp. chopped onion
6 eggs, slightly beaten

3 Tbsp. milk
2 tsp. parsley, minced
½ c. diced SPAM®
salt and pepper to taste
¼ c. Parmesan cheese

In a medium sized skillet, saute mushrooms, zucchini, and onions in 3 Tbsp. of butter for about 3 minutes. Transfer to a bowl. Combine eggs, milk, salt and pepper, and SPAM®. Heat 2 Tbsp. butter in skillet over medium heat. Pour in egg mixture and cook until mixture is partially set, but still soft on top. Sprinkle top of eggs with mushrooms, zucchini, onions, and cheese. Place the skillet in a 450 degree oven for about 4 minutes, or until eggs are set. Garnish with parsley.

If you don't have an oven-proof handle on a skillet, wrap several layers of foil around it for protection.

"Forget the gourmet stuff . . . serve SPAM® 'n' eggs 'n' rice!"

SPAM® McLolly

SPAM®, sliced
eggs, scrambled or fried

slices of cheddar cheese
English muffins, toasted

Fry **SPAM®** until nice and brown. Prepare eggs as desired. Place **SPAM®**, eggs, and cheese between English muffins.

Lolly Saari's special breakfast ... because McDonald's doesn't serve **SPAM®**.

SPAM® Quiche

1 9-inch pie shell (frozen or your own recipe)
1 Tbsp. butter or margarine
½ c. SPAM®, cut into ½ inch strips
¼ c. onion, sliced
1 c. grated cheese (Swiss, Cheddar, or Jack)

1 c. broccoli, sliced and parboiled
3 eggs
1 can (12 oz.) evaporated milk
½ tsp. salt
¼ tsp. nutmeg
dash of tabasco sauce
Parmesan cheese

Bake pie crust in 450 degree oven for 5 minutes. Set aside.

Parboil broccoli and drain. Saute SPAM® and onions in butter until onions are limp. Fill pie crust with SPAM®, onions, broccoli, and grated cheese. Beat together eggs, evaporated milk, nutmeg, salt, and tabasco sauce. Pour egg mixture over the ingredients in pie crust. Sprinkle with Parmesan cheese. Bake at 425 degrees for 10 minutes. Reduce oven temperature to 350 degrees and bake 20 minutes or until quiche is set and golden brown. Cool 10 minutes before slicing.

Even Haoles who say they hate SPAM® like this quiche.

"And what makes you so sure there's SPAM® in Wisconsin?"

Fried Saimin

1 pkg. saimin, with seasoning pkg.
2 Tbsp. oil
½ c. SPAM®, slivered

about 2 c. of vegetables of your choice: bean sprouts, sliced onions, slivered carrots and string beans, etc.

Boil saimin for 3-5 minutes in water. Drain. Heat oil and stir fry SPAM® and vegetables. Add saimin and ½ pkg. of seasonings. Toss together. Add more seasoning if necessary.

Super easy and a change from the soupy saimin.

Gon Lo Mein with SPAM®

2 pkg. (10 oz.) ready to eat chow mein noodles
3 Tbsp. oyster sauce
1 Tbsp. sesame oil
2 Tbsp. oil
1 pkg. beansprouts
1 small carrot, cut in matchstick slivers
1 small onion, sliced

1 c. Chinese peas (or sliced green beans)
3 stalks green onion, cut in 1-inch lengths
1 c. SPAM® cut in matchstick slivers
½ tsp. salt
1 Tbsp. sugar
2 Tbsp. oyster sauce

Place noodles in a 9 x 13 inch pan. Sprinkle with oyster sauce and sesame oil and heat in a 300 degree oven for about 10 minutes.

Heat oil in a wok or large skillet and stir fry remaining ingredients. Toss together with noodles. Garnish with Chinese parsley, if desired.

"*It must be a local delicacy.*"

SPAM® Fried Rice

leftover rice, about 4 cups (cooked)
1½ c. SPAM®, diced

1 egg
1 Tbsp. shoyu
3 stalks green onion, chopped

Fry **SPAM®** in a bit of oil in a skillet. Turn heat to low and add rice. Mix egg with shoyu and add to the rice and **SPAM®**. Add chopped green onions just before serving.

Good with fried eggs.

Chow Fun

2 Tbsp. oil
1 clove garlic, minced
1 can **SPAM®**, cut in thin strips
2 stalks celery, thinly sliced
½ small onion, thinly sliced

Seasoning:
1 thin slice ginger, crushed
1 tsp. sugar
1½ Tbsp. shoyu

Garnish:
roasted sesame seeds
Chinese parsley, chopped

1 pkg. (12 oz.) bean sprouts
3 stalks green onion, cut in 1-inch lengths
1 pkg. (7-8 oz.) chow fun noodles, boiled and drained

Put oil in wok or large skillet. Heat; add garlic. Add ingredients in the following order and stir fry: **SPAM®**, seasonings, and vegetables. Do not overcook vegetables. Add noodles and toss together. Sprinkle with parsley and sesame seeds before serving.

Udon Chow Fun

2 pkg. udon noodles, boiled and drained
1 Tbsp. oil
½ can **SPAM®**, cut into thin strips
1 pkg. (12 oz.) bean sprouts

1 carrot, cut into thin strips
3-5 stalks green onion, cut in 1 inch
  lengths
salt to taste
2 tsp. shoyu

Stir fry **SPAM®** and vegetables in oil (use a large skillet or a wok). Toss noodles with **SPAM®** and veggies and add seasonings.

This is Matsuko Kubo's recipe, and is different because it uses Japanese udon noodles instead of chow fun noodles.

SPAM® Sushi (Hand Roll)

SPAM® strips, cooked Sato-Shoyu style, p. 14
sushi rice
nori

cucumber sticks
radish sprouts
takuwan strips
wasabi

Sushi Rice:
Wash and cook 3 cups Calrose rice. While still hot, season with vinegar sauce, or use packaged sushi mix such as Sushi-No-Ko.

Vinegar Sauce:
½ c. Japanese rice vinegar
½ c. sugar
1 tsp. salt

Cook until sugar dissolves. Cool. Sprinkle half of vinegar sauce over hot rice; mix gently. Add more vinegar sauce to taste. Or, follow instructions on packaged mix.

To assemble sushi:
Cut a sheet of nori in half. Place nori on your left hand; add a small amount of rice. Add SPAM® and all or some of the other ingredients. Wrap nori around the filling and roll from left to right.

Super Macaroni and Cheese

1 box (7¼ oz.) macaroni and cheese
   dinner
2 cloves garlic, minced

3 Tbsp. butter
1 c. sliced mushrooms
½ can **SPAM®**, cubed
grated cheddar cheese (optional)

Prepare macaroni and cheese according to directions on box.

Melt butter in a skillet. Add garlic, mushrooms, and cubed **SPAM®** and cook until mushrooms are soft. Add mushrooms and **SPAM®** to prepared macaroni and cheese. Place in a casserole and sprinkle top with additional grated cheese if desired. Bake for 25-30 minutes in a 350 degree oven.

Little kids love this dish which was contributed by David Hanaike.

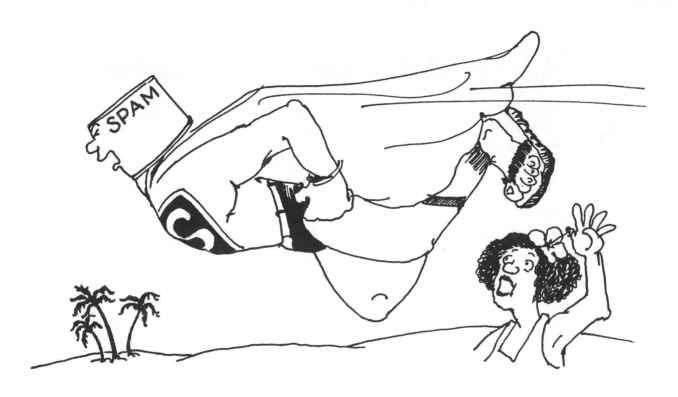

"It's SUPERSPAM®!"

SPAM® and Cauliflower Casserole

1 head cauliflower
1½ c. diced **SPAM**®
2 stalks green onion, thinly sliced
1 c. sour cream

½ tsp. paprika
dash of pepper
dash of nutmeg
1 egg
1 c. cheddar cheese, grated

Break cauliflower up and cook in salted water. Drain. Grease a casserole and make alternate layers of cauliflower and **SPAM**®. Combine all other ingredients, except cheese. Pour over cauliflower and **SPAM**®. Cover and bake at 350 degrees for 30 minutes. Remove cover, top with cheese and bake another 10 minutes.

SPAM® and Beans

2 cans (15 oz.) pork and beans
1 tsp. dry mustard

2 Tbsp. dark brown sugar
2 Tbsp. catsup
1 c. diced **SPAM®**

Mix all ingredients together. Pour into a casserole and bake at 350 degrees for 30 minutes.

Depression Dinner Party Dish

1 can SPAM®, cubed
1 c. bread crumbs
1 Tbsp. minced onions
1 c. peas

¼ c. pimento (optional)
3 eggs, separated
¼ c. melted butter
½ c. milk
1 c. grated cheddar cheese

Mix first 5 ingredients. Beat egg yolks; add butter and milk and stir into other ingredients. Beat egg whites until fluffy and fold into egg-SPAM® mixture. Pour into an 8 x 12 inch pan, sprinkle with cheese, and bake at 350 degrees for 45 minutes. Serves 8-12.

This recipe contributed by Clarice Cox.

SPAM® Noodles

1 box noodle roni Parmesano
1 can **SPAM®**, cubed
1 Tbsp. butter

2 Tbsp. minced onion
2 Tbsp. celery, chopped
1 Tbsp. parsley, minced

Cook noodles as directed on package. Melt butter in a saucepan and saute onions and celery. Fry **SPAM®** for 1 minute then add to noodles and vegetables. Add parsley last.

SPAM® and Vegetable Medley

3 Tbsp. oil
2 medium Maui onions or sweet Spanish onions, cut in wedges
3 medium potatoes, sliced ¼ inch thick

1 can SPAM®, cut in half and then sliced ½ inch thick
⅓ c. water
½ tsp. thyme
½ tsp. sugar
1 pkg. (10 oz.) frozen cut green beans

Heat oil in a skillet and saute onions and potatoes until lightly browned. Add remaining ingredients, except for beans. Cover; simmer for 10 minutes, stirring occasionally. Add beans and cook 10 minutes, or until all vegetables are tender.

Quick SPAM® Stir Fry

SPAM®, cut in matchstick slivers
veggies . . . any kind

dash of pepper
drop or two of shoyu

Stir fry **SPAM®** with any kind of vegetable. The combinations are endless . . . watercress, cabbage, won bok, beans, Chinese peas, zucchini, bean sprouts, etc. Serve with plenty of hot rice.

This is how you can stretch a can of SPAM® to serve a whole tribe. Use plenty of vegetables, and if you want more protein, add some cubed tofu.

SPAM® With Veggies

1 can SPAM®
1 pkg. bean sprouts
1 bunch broccoli

2 beef boullion cubes
water
2 Tbsp. cornstarch

Slice **SPAM®** and fry. Add sliced broccoli and bean sprouts and stir fry. Dissolve 2 beef boullion cubes in ½-¾ c. water. Add 2 Tbsp. cornstarch. Add liquid to **SPAM®** and veggies. Sprinkle with pepper. Do not overcook.

This recipe is for folks who like a little gravy with their stir fried food.

Tofu Patties

1 block tofu
½ pkg. chop suey mix or 1½ c. bean
  sprouts
½ carrot, coarsely grated
2 Tbsp. chopped green onion

4 eggs
2 Tbsp. cornstarch
1 tsp. sugar
¼ tsp. pepper
1 c. **SPAM**® sliced in matchstick
  slivers

Squeeze liquid out of tofu. (Use cheesecloth or cut tofu in slices and blot with several layers of paper towel).
Place tofu in a bowl and mash it with a spoon. Add all other ingredients and mix thoroughly. Form patties and fry in 1 Tbsp. oil until golden brown.

Sweet-Sour Tofu and SPAM®

2 Tbsp. oil
1 block firm tofu
1 c. SPAM® sliced in strips
1 slice (¼ inch thick) ginger, crushed
1 c. chicken stock (or use 1 boullion
cube dissolved in 1 c. water)
3 Tbsp. shoyu

¼ c. sugar
¼ c. vinegar
1 carrot, sliced
3 bamboo shoots, sliced
1 small onion, sliced
¼ c. Chinese peas, or frozen peas
¼ c. water
2 tsp. cornstarch

Cut tofu in thick slices and drain on paper towels. Heat oil in wok or skillet. Fry
SPAM® with ginger. Add vinegar, stock, shoyu, sugar, and cook a few minutes.
Add tofu and vegetables and cook a few more minutes. Thicken sauce with
cornstarch mixed with water.

Other vegetables may be substituted.

Sweet-Sour SPAM®

1 Tbsp. oil
1 can SPAM®

1 onion, cubed
2 bell peppers, cubed

Sauce:

1 Tbsp. oil
1 c. pineapple juice
½ c. brown sugar
1 Tbsp. shoyu

1 Tbsp. vinegar
3 Tbsp. cornstarch
6 Tbsp. water
1 c. pineapple chunks or tidbits

Stir fry peppers, onion, and SPAM® in oil.
In a saucepan combine oil, pineapple juice, and sugar. Heat. Mix together cornstarch, shoyu, vinegar, and water. Add to hot juice, stirring until mixture thickens. Add the SPAM® and vegetables and heat thoroughly. Add pineapple just before serving.

SPAM® and Eggplant

1 can **SPAM®**
3 long eggplants

2 Tbsp. shoyu
½ red chili pepper
2 Tbsp. oil

Slice **SPAM®** into strips. Cut eggplants into diagonal slices. Heat oil in frying pan. Cook eggplants until done. Add **SPAM®** and remove pan from heat. Then add chili pepper and shoyu.

Mama takes a vote on the dinner menu.

SPAM®, String Beans, and Eggs

1 Tbsp. oil
½ can **SPAM®**, cut in matchstick
   slivers

1 pkg. (8 oz.) string beans, thinly
   sliced
3-4 eggs
salt and pepper to taste

Put oil in skillet and stir fry **SPAM®** and string beans. Do not overcook the beans. Break eggs into a small bowl and beat with a fork. Pour eggs over **SPAM®** and beans and cook until eggs are set. Add salt and pepper to taste.

"Ho, so ono!"   Josephine Kawakami

SPAM® and Popping Peas

1 can SPAM®, diced
1 large can (1 lb. 12 oz.) whole
  tomatoes

1 pkg. dry onion soup mix
½ pkg. medium egg noodles
1 pkg. frozen peas

Fry **SPAM**® cubes for a few minutes. Add soup mix and tomatoes. Mash the tomatoes with a spoon. Add noodles (uncooked) and cook until soft. Add peas and cook a few minutes. Do not overcook peas. They should pop in your mouth.

This recipe is adapted from the original Popping Peas in my first book, Easy Cooking the Island Way.

SPAM® and Peas

1 can **SPAM®**
1 pkg. (10 oz.) frozen peas

1 can (8 oz.) tomato sauce
pepper to taste

Dice **SPAM®** and fry in a little oil until brown. Add peas and tomato sauce. Simmer for 5 minutes.

Eat on top hot rice.

67

SPAM® Stuffed Hasu (Lotus Root)

2 hasu sections, each about 5 inches long
1 can SPAM®, ground
dash of pepper
1 clove garlic, minced

1 Tbsp. green onion, minced
½ tsp. crushed toasted sesame seeds
flour
2 eggs, slightly beaten
oil for frying

Peel hasu and slice crosswise into ¼ inch thick slices. Combine SPAM®, pepper, garlic, green onion, and sesame seeds. Place about 1 Tbsp. of the mixture on hasu slices and press. Dip stuffed hasu in flour, shake off excess, then dip in egg. Fry, SPAM® side down in a small amount of hot oil. Turn over and brown other side.

Dipping Sauce.

¼ c. sugar
¼ c. shoyu
2 Tbsp. mirin (Japanese sweet rice wine)

1-2 cloves garlic, minced
1 red chili pepper, thinly sliced (or use red pepper flakes)

Miso SPAM® With Vegetables

½ c. water
2 Tbsp. sugar
¼ c. miso

½ can SPAM®, cubed
2 long eggplants, sliced diagonally, 1 inch thick
1 large bell pepper

Slice eggplant and soak in water for 15 minutes. In a pan, make sauce out of water, sugar and miso. When it is bubbly, add SPAM® and drained eggplant. Cover and cook for a few minutes over low heat until eggplant is almost tender. Add cubed pepper and cook until it is tender but not mushy. Serve with hot rice.

"But was on sale!"

SPAM® and Daikon

½ can **SPAM®**, cut into thin strips
3 daikon, cut in julienne strips

1½ Tbsp. brown sugar
1 Tbsp. mirin
1 Tbsp. shoyu

Saute **SPAM®** and daikon in a bit of oil. Add seasonings and cook until daikon is tender but not mushy.

This recipe comes from Mrs. Higuchi, the famous cook from Maui, who now lives in Aiea.

Eggplant (or Zucchini) and Spam® Tempura

1 can SPAM®
4 eggplants (long type) or 4 zucchini

Oil for frying

Batter:

1 c. Bisquick
1 c. cornstarch
1 tsp. salt

1 c. water
1 egg
drop of yellow food coloring

Cut eggplants or zucchini into 3-inch lengths. Slice each piece lengthwise, but not completely through (so that vegetable remains attached at the bottom). Cut SPAM® into ¼-inch slices and then in half. Insert SPAM® in eggplant or zucchini and fasten with a toothpick.

Combine batter ingredients and blend.
Dip eggplant or zucchini into batter and deep fry in oil that has been heated to 365 degrees. Fry until golden brown. Drain on paper towels and remove toothpicks. Serve with shoyu.

"Stop acting human, George!"

73

Veggie and SPAM® Tempura

1 can SPAM®, cut into matchstick
  slivers
oil for frying

1 (8 oz.) pkg. green beans, sliced
  diagonally into slivers
1 carrot, cut into matchstick slivers
1 small onion, thinly sliced

Batter: Use same batter as for Eggplant and SPAM® Tempura, p. 72

Combine **SPAM®** and veggies. Make batter and add veggies to the batter. Heat oil. Using chopsticks, tongs, or fingers, grab a small portion of veggie-batter and drop into hot oil. Fry until golden brown. Drain on paper towels.

SPAM® and Kim Chee Chun

1 can SPAM®, cut into squares
won bok kim chee, stalks only, rinsed
green onion stalks, cut in 1 inch pieces

celery, cut into thin strips
3-4 eggs
flour
oil for frying

Marinade:

2 Tbsp. shoyu
1 Tbsp. sugar

2 tsp sesame seeds
1 clove garlic, minced
1 Tbsp. oil

Soak SPAM® and vegetables in marinade for about 1 hour then skewer on long cocktail toothpicks, alternating SPAM® between the vegetables. Dredge in some flour and then dip into beaten eggs. Fry in about 2-3 Tbsp. oil over medium heat. Lightly brown on both sides; cool. Remove toothpicks and cut into squares. Serve with vinegar-shoyu sauce.

Vinegar-shoyu sauce: ½ c. Japanese vinegar
2 Tbsp. shoyu
1 clove garlic, minced

Korean Style SPAM®

1 can **SPAM®**, sliced in ½-inch slivers   1 small onion, sliced
1 (12 oz.) jar of Kim Chee   2 tsp. shoyu

Brown **SPAM®** slices in a skillet.
Place Kim Chee in a strainer or colander and rinse with water. Drain well. Add Kim Chee, onion, and shoyu to **SPAM®** and cook about 2 minutes.

Lloyd Pak, who gave me this recipe, says this dish is also good with sliced zucchini and tofu added.

The call of the kim chee and SPAM®.

Corned Beef

Sardines

Vienna Sausage

Corned Beef and Onions

1 Tbsp. oil
1 can corned beef

1 large onion, sliced
pepper to taste

Heat oil in skillet. Put ingredients in skillet and stir together until onions are done.

Corned Beef and Onions, Sato-Shoyu (Sugar-Shoyu)

Follow above recipe, except add 3 Tbsp. sugar, 3 Tbsp. shoyu, and 2 Tbsp. water.

Corned Beef, Onions, and Potatoes

1 Tbsp. oil,
2 potatoes peeled, cut in half and sliced
  ¼ inch thick
1 can corned beef

1 onion, sliced
2 Tbsp. sugar
2 Tbsp. shoyu
¼ c. water
chopped green onions for garnish

Fry sliced potatoes in oil until light brown. Remove from pan and drain on paper towels. In the same pan, fry onions and corned beef. Add seasonings and water. Return potatoes to the pan; cover and cook until potatoes are tender. Garnish with green onions.

This recipe came from a Maui woman who had 8 children to feed. By adding more potatoes and some veggies, she was able to make a meal out of one can of corned beef.

Mrs. Bozo gives a lesson on how to feed a family of 4 on $10.00 a week.

Quick Corned Beef and Cabbage

1 can corned beef

1 small head cabbage, cut in chunks
salt and pepper to taste

Put corned beef in a pan and break it up. Cook over medium heat for about a minute; add cabbage, salt and pepper. Cover and cook until cabbage is limp, but not mushy.

Some people add a bit of sugar and shoyu to this instead of salt and pepper.

Fried Corned Beef and Cabbage

1 can corned beef

¼ c. flour
1 small head cabbage, cut in wedges

Refrigerate corned beef to make it solid. Slice it and roll in flour. Fry in some oil. Boil cabbage, drain well. Place corned beef on top of cabbage and serve.

Corned Beef and Cabbage Salad

4 potatoes, cooked, peeled and diced
3 Tbsp. oil
2 Tbsp. vinegar
½ tsp. celery seed
½ tsp. salt
1 tsp. sugar
1 can corned beef, chilled and cubed

1 c. finely shredded cabbage
3 stalks green onion, thinly sliced
2 tsp. prepared mustard
¾ c. mayonnaise
¼ tsp. salt
pepper to taste
parsley for garnish

Combine oil, vinegar, celery seed, ½ tsp. salt, and sugar. Pour over warm potatoes; toss and chill.
Before serving, add all other ingredients. Toss together and garnish with parsley.

Corned Beef Spread

8 oz. pkg. of cream cheese
2 Tbsp. mayonnaise
2 Tbsp. Dijon style mustard

1 can corned beef
½ c. finely chopped radishes
2 stalks green onion, minced

Mix together cream cheese, mayonnaise, and mustard until fluffy. Fold in corned beef, radishes, and green onions. Cover and chill several hours. Serve with rye rounds or crackers.

An easy pupu.

Corned Beef Sandwich Filling

1 can corned beef
1 Tbsp. chopped onion
pepper

1 Tbsp. pickle relish
1 Tbsp. prepared mustard
mayonnaise (enough to moisten)

Mix all ingredients together and spread on bread.

Ice Chest Corned Beef Spread

Cabbage, finely shredded
Mayonnaise

1 can corned beef
1 ziploc bag

Put finely shredded cabbage and some mayonnaise in a ziploc bag. Put it in your ice chest. Take 1 can corned beef and bread. When you get ready to eat, open corned beef and mix it with the cabbage and mayonnaise in the ziploc bag. Spread on bread.

"This is a convenient way to make sandwiches when you are on a picnic or rocking on a fishing boat." George Kashiwa

Reuben Sandwich

Rye bread
Russian dressing
canned corned beef

1 can sauerkraut
sliced Swiss cheese
butter

Spread slices of rye bread with Russian dressing, pile on some sliced corned beef, pile on some sauerkraut, top with a slice of Swiss cheese. Cover with another slice of bread. Butter top and bottom of the sandwich and toast in a toaster oven or in a cast iron skillet.

Corned Beef Omelet

For each omelet:
1 Tbsp. butter
2-3 eggs

1 Tbsp. milk
¼ c. corned beef
pepper to taste

Mix eggs, milk, corned beef, and pepper together with a fork. Melt butter in a small skillet or omelet pan. When it is sizzling, add egg mixture. Cook until almost set and fold over.

Corned Beef Hash Patties

1 can corned beef
2 medium potatoes, diced

½ small onion, minced
salt and pepper to taste

Cook the diced potatoes in water until soft (do not overcook). Drain well. In a bowl, mash the potatoes, corned beef, and onions together. Form into patties and brown in some hot oil or butter in a frying pan.

If you go to Okazu-ya, you might find that the corned beef hash patties are WHITE because they use plenty potatoes and little bit corned beef! Randy Higa reports that his Ma makes them white too.

Mrs. Higuchi's Corned Beef Patties

Follow basic recipe for corned beef hash patties, except add 1 egg, 1 carrot, shredded, and about ½ c. of thinly sliced string beans.

Corned Beef and Vegetable Patties

1 can corned beef
1 c. bread crumbs
1 medium onion, chopped
1 medium carrot, grated

leftover vegetables (beans, celery, bean sprouts)
1 egg
salt and pepper to taste

Mix all ingredients together. Form into patties and fry in some oil or bacon fat.

Papakolea
Hawaiian Goulash

1 can **SPAM®** cubed
1 can corned beef
1 small onion, chopped

1 pkg. (12 oz.) frozen mixed
  vegetables
1 can (8 oz.) tomato sauce
dash of pepper

Put all ingredients in a pan. Heat and eat on top rice.

Corned Beef Crescents

1 can (12 oz.) corned beef
1 small potato, finely cubed
½ c. chopped onions
1 c. frozen peas and carrots
¼ tsp. salt

¼ tsp. pepper
1 Tbsp. Dijon mustard
1 egg
1 box crust dough, prepared as
   directed (or make your own pie crust
   for a 2-crust pie)

Makes 8

Prepare pie crust according to directions on box and divide into 8 equal portions. On a lightly floured surface, roll out each portion of dough to form a 7-inch circle. Set aside on waxed paper.

In a bowl, mix together corned beef, vegetables, and seasonings, and egg. Place about ¾ cup of meat mixture on half of each pie crust circle. Fold over to make a half circle. Moisten edge and seal with a fork. Poke holes on top of each crescent with a fork. Beat 1 egg yolk and brush on top of each crescent. Place on an ungreased baking sheet. Bake 350 degrees for 45 minutes or until golden brown.

If desired, serve with a sauce made out of:
1 c. sour cream   1 Tbsp. Dijon mustard   dash of pepper
1 Tbsp. lemon juice   ¼ tsp. salt

Confetti Corned Beef

1 can corned beef
1 (10 oz.) pkg. frozen peas and carrots

½ small onion, chopped
salt and pepper to taste

Saute corned beef over medium heat in a skillet. Add peas, carrots and onions and cook until done, but not mushy. Season with salt and pepper.

If you have a bigger tribe to feed, add 1 can of corn!

Haole Manapua

Makes 16

1 can corned beef
¾ c. diced cheddar cheese
¼ c. mayonnaise
1 Tbsp. pickle relish
1 Tbsp. minced onion

1 tsp. Worcestershire sauce
1 tsp. sugar
2 cans refrigerated crescent rolls
1 egg, beaten
sesame seeds

Combine corned beef, cheese, mayonnaise, pickle relish, onion, Worcestershire sauce, and sugar. Set aside. Separate crescent rolls and place a spoonful of the corned beef mixture on the wide end of each triangle. Wrap dough around filling, pinching edges to seal each bun. Place on cookie sheets. Brush with egg and sprinkle with sesame seeds. Bake at 350 degrees for 20-25 minutes.

Corned Beef Manapua

Makes 16

1 can corned beef
2 Tbsp. shoyu
¼ c. brown sugar
½ tsp. grated ginger (or ½ tsp. ground
   ginger)
1 Tbsp. sake or wine

1 egg
1 can (8 oz.) water chestnuts, minced
2 stalks green onions, minced
2 cans refrigerated crescent rolls
1 beaten egg and sesame seeds for
   topping

Mix corned beef, shoyu, brown sugar, ginger, sake, water chestnuts, green onions, and egg together. Open crescent rolls and unroll each piece. Place about a tablespoon of filling on wide end of each roll; roll it up, forming it into a bun and pinching dough to enclose filling. Place on a cookie sheet. Brush with beaten egg and sprinkle with sesame seeds. Bake in 350 degree oven for 20-25 minutes.

Island folks living on the mainland: now you can make your own manapua!

Creamed Corned Beef

1 can cream based soup, such as cream
  of mushroom
½ can milk

dash of pepper
1 can corned beef
1 c. frozen vegetables such as peas
  and carrots or mixed vegetables

Heat soup, milk, pepper. Add corned beef and vegetables. Serve on top hot rice.

Portuguese Tacos

½ Portuguese sausage (about 6 oz.),
  diced
1 can corned beef
¼ c. chopped onion
½ pkg. taco seasoning

½-¾ c. water
prepared taco shells (10-12)
chopped lettuce
diced tomatoes
shredded cheese

Fry Portuguese sausage in a pan; drain on paper towels. Remove any fat from pan and add the corned beef, Portuguese sausage, and onions. Cook until onions are tender; add taco seasoning and water and cook 5-10 minutes. Fill taco shells and top with lettuce, tomatoes, and cheese.

You may omit Portuguese sausage if you wish (then these won't be Portuguese tacos) and add more taco seasoning. The idea for Portuguese tacos came from David Hanaike.

Corned Beef Enchiladas

2 Tbsp. butter or margarine
1 can corned beef
½ onion, chopped
1 clove garlic, minced
1 can cream of mushroom soup
1 c. milk

½ tsp. cumin
½ c. sour cream
1 Tbsp. flour
2 Tbsp. diced green chilies
5-6 flour tortillas
½ c. grated cheese

In skillet, heat corned beef, onion, and garlic in butter until onion is tender. Set aside in a bowl. In same skillet, combine soup, milk, and cumin. Heat until bubbly. Mix together flour and sour cream; add to soup mixture. Stir ⅓ c. of the sauce into the corned beef mixture. Stir chilies into remaining sauce in skillet. Fill each tortilla with about ¼ c. of corned beef mixture. Roll up and place in an oven proof casserole. Pour sauce on top. Bake in 350 degree oven for about 25 minutes. Sprinkle with cheese before serving.

Corned Beef Noodle Casserole

1 can corned beef
1 can cream of mushroom soup
1 c. milk
½ c. chopped onion

1 c. cheddar cheese, grated
¼ tsp. pepper
8 oz. medium egg noodles, boiled and
drained

Mix together cream of mushroom soup, milk, and onion. Grease a casserole and make alternate layers of noodles, corned beef, soup mixture, and cheese. Sprinkle with pepper and bake at 350 degrees for 30-40 minutes.

A good busy day casserole that can be made the night before and refrigerated for the next day.

"Auwe! SPAM®, corned beef, and sardines on sale!"

Sardines and Eggs

1 can sardines, drained and mashed
3-4 eggs
salt and pepper to taste

Mix ingredients together. Put a little butter or oil in a skillet and scramble eggs and sardines.

Lomi Sardines

1 can sardines, drained
1 tomato, diced
2 Tbsp. Maui onion, chopped

2 stalks green onion, minced
½ tsp. Hawaiian salt
½ tsp. chili pepper flakes
1 tsp. vinegar

Lomi all ingredients together. Chill and eat with poi or rice.

When you're too poor to buy salmon, use sardines . . . ono!

Sardine Buns

3 cans sardines, drained
1 lb. cheddar cheese, grated
1 can (8 oz.) tomato sauce
1 Tbsp. Worcestershire sauce
1 tsp. salt

½ tsp. pepper
½ c. chopped ripe olives
¼ c. chopped onion
1 c. chopped celery
2 Tbsp. pimento
12 Hamburger buns

Mix all ingredients, except buns, together. Fill each bun with sardine filling. Wrap in foil and bake at 300 degrees for 30 minutes. Remove foil and bake 10 minutes longer.

Sardine Spread

1 can sardines, drained and mashed
2 Tbsp. catsup
1 tsp. Dijon mustard

1 tsp. Worcestershire sauce
1 Tbsp. minced onion
2 tsp. lemon juice
dash of salt and pepper

Mix all ingredients together. Spread on crackers, or use as a sandwich filling.

Sardines and Onions

1 can sardines, drained
1 onion, sliced or 3 stalks green onion,
    sliced

1 Tbsp. shoyu
2 tsp. sugar
1 Tbsp. white wine or water

Heat all ingredients in a small pan. Eat with hot rice.

Simple, satisfying plantation food!

Sardines with Somen

1 can sardines
shoyu to taste

6 stalks green onion, cut in 1 inch
    lengths
1 pkg. somen, cooked and drained

Empty sardines into frying pan. Place on medium heat; add onions and cook 2-3 minutes. Put somen into pan and toss together. Add shoyu to taste and eat!

Filipino Style Sardines and Long Rice

1 Tbsp. oil
1 tomato, cubed
1 clove garlic, minced
½ onion, chopped

2 cans (5.5 oz.) tomato sardines with chilies
2 bundles long rice, soaked in warm water
4-5 c. water

Saute tomatoes, garlic, and onions in oil. Drain long rice and cut in half. Add long rice and all other ingredients to tomatoes and onions. Cook until long rice is translucent and tender, adding more water if necessary. Add salt to taste, if desired.

This recipe comes from the files of the famous cook, Mrs. Agtarap.

Tomato Sardine Salad

1 can (15 oz. oval) tomato sardines
6 large heads Manoa lettuce

1 Tbsp. shoyu
2 Tbsp. toasted sesame seeds
salt to taste

Wash lettuce and drain well. Combine other ingredients and toss with lettuce just before serving.

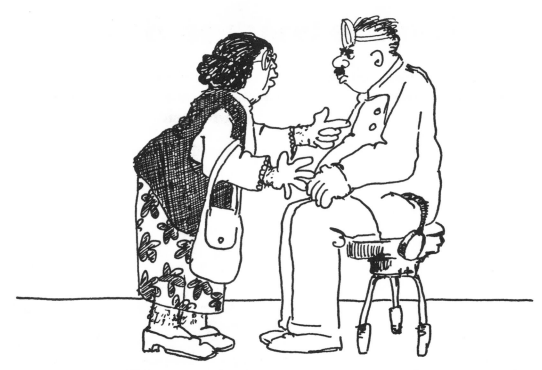

"Have you had your sardines today?"
(Okinawan secret to good health).

Sardine Salad

2 peeled, sliced potatoes (cooked)
1 (8 oz.) pkg. green beans, blanched and chilled
1 bunch romaine, torn in large pieces
2 cans sardines, drained

1 cucumber, diced
4 tomatoes, cut in quarters
3 hard boiled eggs, sliced
½ c. olives
3 Tbsp. parsley, minced

Dressing:
Mix and chill the following:
½ c. lemon juice
1 Tbsp. Dijon mustard
1 Tbsp. chopped capers
½ tsp. sugar

½ tsp. salt
¾ c. oil
1 clove garlic, minced
¼ tsp. pepper
1 stalk minced green onions

Line a large platter with romaine and spread potatoes in a layer. Spoon some dressing on top of potatoes. Arrange all other ingredients in an attractive pattern over potatoes. Spoon remaining dressing on top and chill for 2 hours before serving.

Sardine-Okara Patties

2 c. okara (tofu residue)
1 can sardines, with oil, mashed
½ tsp. salt
1 Tbsp. sugar
2 eggs

2 Tbsp. cornstarch
2 stalks green onion, minced
1 small carrot, minced
flour
oil

Mix together all ingredients, except flour and oil. Make patties, roll in flour and fry in oil.

Sardines and Tofu

1 can sardines
1 small block tofu, cubed
2 Tbsp. shoyu
1 Tbsp. sugar

2 Tbsp. white wine or water
½ pkg. bean sprouts
2 stalks green onion, cut into 1 inch
  lengths

Heat all ingredients in a pan. Do not overcook veggies.

A cheap high protein meal!

Sardine and Tofu Souffle

1 can sardines, drained and mashed
1 zucchini, coarsely grated
1 carrot, coarsely grated
1 pkg. bean sprouts

1 block tofu
8 eggs, beaten
1 tsp. salt
oyster sauce

Grate zucchini and carrot. Cut tofu into slices and blot each piece with paper towels. Mash tofu and add all ingredients except oyster sauce. Pour into a greased casserole or a loaf pan. Bake at 350 degrees for 45-55 minutes. Spread oyster sauce on top before serving.

This is a healthy dish ... tastes good, too!

TOFU SOUFFLE?

Mabel's Kim Chee Sardines

1 can (15 oz. oval) tomato sardines
1 jar (12 oz.) won bok kim chee
1 bell pepper, sliced

1 Maui onion, sliced
1 Tbsp. sugar
1 Tbsp. shoyu
2 tsp. sesame seeds

Drain liquid from kim chee. Rinse with water, if you don't like your food too hot. Chop the kim chee. Combine all ingredients in a pan and simmer until vegetables are tender. Serve with hot rice.

This recipe from Maui's Mabel Shin.

Sardine and Warabi (Fern Shoots)

2 cans sardines   shoyu
1 bunch warabi, cut in 2-inch lengths   chili pepper

Put sardines (including oil) in a pan. Add warabi, shoyu to taste, and a bit of chili pepper. Cook until warabi is tender.

Warabi grows on the Big Island, but you can sometimes find it at open markets and in Chinatown.

Sardines and Eggplant

3-4 long eggplants
1 can sardine

1 Tbsp. shoyu
1 Tbsp. sugar

Slice eggplants lengthwise in half and cut into 3 inch pieces. Open sardines, pour oil from can into frying pan and cook the eggplants. When almost done, add shoyu, sugar, and sardines. Cook 3 minutes.

Sardine-Miso Udon

1 pkg. (4 oz.) Osaka Udon
5-6 c. water
½ c. miso

1 can sardines, rinsed in water, bones removed
1 bunch pak choy or Swiss chard, blanched and cut in 1 inch pieces

Parboil udon in 1 quart water for 4 minutes. Do not use seasoning package at this time. Drain noodles.

Bring 5-6 cups of water to a boil; add miso and stir until dissolved. Add sardines and half of the udon seasoning package. Add udon and cook until tender. Add vegetables just before serving.

This dish becomes less soupy as it sits, so if you want soup, eat it immediately.

Sardine Ozoni

1 can sardines, rinsed in warm water,
   drained, mid-bone removed
6 c. water
1 pkg. dashi-no-moto (soup seasoning)
½ tsp. salt

1 tsp. shoyu
3 large shiitake mushrooms, soaked in
   water and sliced
½ daikon, thinly sliced
½ bunch mizuna, cut 1 inch long
6 small mochi

Bring sardines, water, dashi-no-moto, salt and shoyu to a boil. Add mushrooms
and daikon and cook until daikon is tender. Add mizuna and mochi just before
serving.

Ozoni is traditionally eaten by Japanese on New Year's Day.

"But Hiroshi, you know we always eat ozoni on New Year's Day!"

"That SPAM® thinks he's big deal!"

Vienna Sausage Pupus

½ c. flour
⅓ c. cornmeal
1 tsp. baking powder
1 tsp. dry mustard
½ tsp. salt

1 egg
1 c. milk
1 Tbsp. oil
3 cans (9 oz.) Vienna Sausage
oil for frying

Mix dry ingredients together. Add egg, milk, and 1 Tbsp. oil and stir until blended. Dip each sausage in batter and deep fry until golden brown. Insert a toothpick in each one and serve with sauce.

Sauce:

½ c. sugar
½ c. water
½ c. vinegar

3 Tbsp. catsup
3 Tbsp. shoyu
½ tsp. salt

Bring all ingredients to a boil, pour into a small bowl and serve with pupus.

Polka-Dot Pancakes

2 c. flour
4 tsp. baking powder
1 tsp. salt
1 Tbsp. sugar

1 egg
1 c. milk
¼ c. oil
1-2 cans Vienna sausage (5 oz.), sliced
    horizontally into rounds

Make batter (or use pancake mix). For each pancake, place 4-5 rounds of sausage on griddle and pour pancake batter over them. Brown; flip over and cook the other side.

Kids love this!

Pokey-Pokey or Filipino Scrambled Eggs

1 Tbsp. oil
1 clove garlic, minced
1 large long eggplant, boiled and
   mashed

1 can (5 oz.) Vienna sausage, mashed
   with a fork
3-4 eggs, beaten
garlic salt to taste

Heat oil in skillet and fry minced garlic.
Mix all other ingredients together and pour into pan.
Scramble and cook until done.

Mrs. Agtarap (of Sardine and Long Rice fame) makes eggs this way.

Puukolii Pork 'N' Beans

1 can (15 oz.) pork and beans
1 can (9 oz.) Vienna sausage

1 can SPAM®, diced
1 can corn (if you want color)

Put all ingredients in a pan and heat. Pour on top rice and eat. Especially good when you're camping on the beach.

This recipe contributed by Richard Anbe, a living reminder of the hazards of eating Puukolii Pork 'N' Beans!

GLOSSARY

Aburage: Fried tofu.

Chinese fishcake: A fish paste made by scraping the flesh of certain fish. Available at local markets and fish markets.

Chow fun: Wide, flat, Chinese noodles.

Chun: Foods fried in egg and flour (Korean).

Daikon: Japanese radish.

Dashi-no-moto: Packaged seasoning for soups and other Japanese dishes.

Fishcake: see Chinese fishcake.

Fu Young: Mixed up, scrambled; e.g. egg fu young.

Furikake nori: seasoned flaked seaweed used on top of rice.

Gon lo mein: Chinese noodles without gravy.

Hasu: Lotus root.

Kamaboko: Japanese fishcake

Kim chee: Korean pickled vegetables with spicy seasoning.

Long rice: dried, transparent noodles made out of mung bean starch.

Lumpia: Filipino vegetable-meat roll, deep fried.

Manapua: General name given to dumplings filled with meat or sweets.

Mirin: Japanese sweet rice wine.

Miso: Fermented soy bean paste.

Mizuna: Mild flavored Japanese cabbage.

Mochi: Japanese rice cakes traditionally eaten at New Year's.

Musubi: Rice ball.

Nori: Seaweed used to roll sushi.

Okara: Tofu derivative; the residue after soy milk has been pressed out of soybeans.

Okazu-ya: Japanese deli.

Oyster sauce: Chinese seasoning made out of fermented oysters.

Ozoni: Soup with mochi and vegetables traditionally eaten by Japanese on New Year's Day.

Pak choy: Chinese cabbage resembling Swiss chard.

Papakolea: Hawaiian homestead community in Honolulu.

Portagee steak: (Portuguese steak); SPAM®.

Pupu: Appetizer or hor d'oeuvere.

Rice vinegar: Japanese vinegar, milder in flavor than other vinegars.

Saimin: Japanese noodles.

Sato-shoyu: Sugar-shoyu sauce.

Shiitake: Dried Japanese mushrooms.

Shoyu: Soy sauce.

Somen: Thin Japanese noodles.

Stir-fry: Method of cooking quickly over high heat in a small amount of oil.

Sushi-no-ko: Packaged sushi seasoning.

Tempura: Food dipped in batter then deep fried.

Tofu: Soybean curd.

Udon: Thick, flat Japanese noodles.

Ume: Pickled plum.

Wakame: A type of thin, dry seaweed.

Warabi: Edible fern shoots.

Wasabi: Japanese horseradish.

Water chestnut: Small, crunchy tuber used in oriental cookery.

Won bok: Chinese or celery cabbage, often used for making Kim chee.

Won ton: Chinese dumpling filled with meat; may be deep fried or used in soup.

ORDER BLANK

Please send me _____ copies of HAWAII'S SPAM® COOKBOOK
@ $8.95 each*.

I am enclosing my check or money order for $_____ ,
payable to BESS PRESS.

_____
Name (Please Print)

_____
Address

_____
City   State   Zip

*Price includes tax and handling charge. Allow 6-8 weeks for delivery.

BESS PRESS
P.O. BOX 22388
HONOLULU, HI 96823